Exploring Numbers

© Aladdin Books Ltd 1998
Produced by
Aladdin Books Ltd
28 Percy Street
London W1P OLD

*First published in the United States
in 1998 by*
Copper Beech Books,
an imprint of
The Millbrook Press
2 Old New Milford Road
Brookfield, Connecticut
06804

Project Editor: Sally Hewitt
Editor: Liz White
Design: David West Children's Book Design
Designer: Simon Morse
Photography: Roger Vlitos
Illustrator: Tony Kenyon

Printed in Belgium
5 4 3 2 1

**Library of Congress
Cataloging-in-Publication Data**

King, Andrew, 1961-
Exploring numbers / by Andrew King ; illustrated by Tony Kenyon.
p. cm. — (Math for Fun)
Includes index.
Summary: Games and projects introduce the number
system, starting with place value and ending with
the four operations—addition,
subtraction, multiplication, and division.
ISBN 0-7613-0733-8 (pbk.). — ISBN 0-7613-0722-2 (lib. bdg.)
1. Mathematics—Juvenile literature.
[1. Mathematics. 2. Mathematical recreations.]
I. Kenyon, Tony, ill. II. Title.
III. Series: King, Andrew, 1961- Math for fun.
QA40.5.K56 1998   97-41605
513—dc21   CIP AC

MATH *for fun*

Exploring Numbers

Andrew King

Copper Beech Books
Brookfield, Connecticut

CONTENTS

NUMBER FACTS **6**

SUMMING UP **8**

COUNTING DOWN **10**

VALUE YOUR DIGITS! **12**

PLACE YOUR DIGITS **14**

BIG, BIGGER, BIGGEST **16**

SIGN OF THE TIMES **18**

DO THE OPPOSITE **20**

HARD TIMES! **22**

BIG TIME OPERATOR **24**

GAMES GALORE! **26**

PROBLEMS, PROBLEMS... **28**

TIMES TABLES **30**

GLOSSARY **31**

INDEX **32**

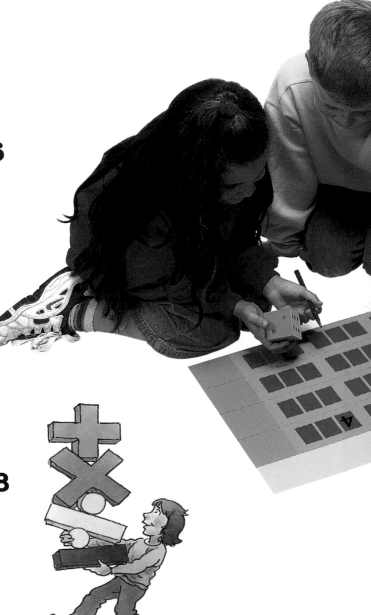

INTRODUCTION

It's amazing what you can do when you know how to count and calculate! You can add, subtract, multiply, and divide numbers with ease. Calculating means figuring something out. People use calculations all the time; they use them to write computer games, build bridges, bake cakes, and even send rockets to the moon!

Try the exciting activities, practical projects, and fun games in this book, and you can have fun learning to calculate at the same time.

● Follow the STEP-BY-STEP INSTRUCTIONS to help you with the activities.

● Use the HELPFUL HINTS for clues about the experiments and games.

● Look at MORE IDEAS for information about other projects.

1 Yellow squares mean this is an easy activity.

2 Blue squares mean this is a medium activity.

3 Red squares mean this is a hard activity.

NUMBER FACTS

When you were younger, you probably learned different ways of **adding** up two numbers to make 10. Being able to remember number facts quickly, like 6+4=10 and also 2+8=10, can be helpful in solving many **arithmetic** problems.

X-RAY VISION!
If you know your number facts to 7 you will be able to do this trick and pretend that you have x-ray vision! For this trick you will need a die. You could make one.

1 Cover a cube with colored paper. Stick on shapes for the "number" spots, or you could draw them on.

2 Throw the die a few times. Each time it comes to rest, make a note of the number that is on the top of the die and the number hidden underneath.

3 Do you notice a pattern? If you can see a pattern you are ready to do the trick! Say to your audience, "I have x-ray vision and I can see through the die to the hidden number!"

HELPFUL HINTS

● The secret to this game is that the opposite sides of the die always add up to **equal** 7. If you see a 3 at the top of the die then the hidden face must be 4 because...

3+4=7

It is a bit like trying to solve a problem like this: 3+?=7.

MORE IDEAS

● This is like the x-ray vision trick. It uses the same pattern. Can you work it out? You need two dice. Place one on top of the other. The top face and the hidden faces in the middle and underneath will add up to... you've got it — 14! That's because 7+7=14. You can say, "I know what all three hidden numbers add up to!"

● What is it here? If you can solve the sum 3+?=14, you can find out.

SUMMING UP

We often use the word **sum** to describe any arithmetic problem. The sum is the total of a list of numbers that have been added together.

FIFTEEN!

Fifteen is quite a tricky game. You need to be good at adding up single digit numbers in your head. Make a game board like this with colored cardboard and you are ready to start.

1 To make two sets of pieces, cut out five circles of colored cardboard and five more of a different color.

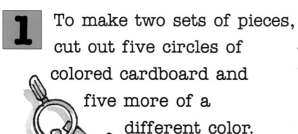

2 Cut a line from the edge to the center of each circle. Slide one cut edge behind the other and stick it in place to make a cone.

← Cut along the dashed line

3 Each player chooses a set of pieces and takes turns to cover one square at a time. The winner of the game is the first person to make a total of 15. If you go over 15, you are "bust" and lose.

HELPFUL HINTS
- If you choose one of the larger numbers to start with, be careful, it is easy to go bust!
- Try and make 15 yourself, but remember, your opponent is also trying to make 15. Can you stop them at the same time?

MORE IDEAS
- Is it better to go first or second in this game? Can you figure out a way to make sure that you win every time?

TWENTY-ONE OR BUST!

- This is another exciting game a little bit like Fifteen. You will need a deck of cards. (The ace counts as 1 or 11. The face cards (Jacks, Queens, and Kings) are worth 10.) Draw two cards from the deck. You can then decide to take another card, or "stay." The object of the game is to get as close to 21 as possible without going over.

COUNTING DOWN

Can you count backward? That's easy! Can you count backward in 2s... from any number? Start on 20. Try 105. What about 1,005? Now try counting backward in 3s! Counting backward is one way of **subtracting,** or taking away.

THE BLACK SPOT!
Some people say that this is an ancient pirate game. You will need to do a lot of backward counting to make sure that you don't lose and walk the plank! Play this with a friend.

1 Find ten white checkers and one black checker for the black spot. Draw pirate faces onto circles of cardboard and stick a face onto each white checker. Stack all the pieces in a column with the black spot at the bottom.

2 Decide who is going first. Each player takes turns to remove either one, two, or three pieces. The object of the game is to make your opponent pick the black spot, so they have to walk the plank!

HELPFUL HINTS

● One way of getting better at this game is to search for winning patterns. If you were the winner, try to remember how you started. What did your opponent do next?

MORE IDEAS

● Is it better to go first or second in this game? How would the way you play the game change if another piece was added to the stack? How would the way you play the game change if you could only remove one or two pieces each turn?

SWEET SIXTEEN

● Another great game like The Black Spot is Sweet Sixteen. It can be played with a calculator. Start with 16 on the display and take turns to subtract 1, 2, or 3. If you manage to leave your opponent with 1 on the display then you have won the game.

VALUE YOUR DIGITS!

Numbers are made up of digits like words are made up of letters. But where a digit is placed in a number affects its value. A two digit number is made up of tens and ones. The 2 in 25 has a value of 20 (two tens), the 5 has a value of 5 (five ones).

DRAW A NUMBER

1 You can design your own numbers to show the value of the digits. You will need some graph paper and some pens, pencils, paint... or whatever you like to help with your design.

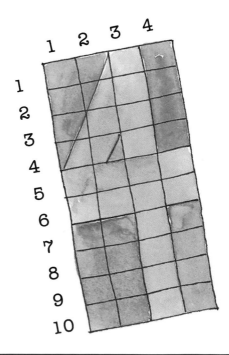

2 Choose a two digit number — what about 46? Draw a rectangle of 40 small squares for the 4 digit and a rectangle of 6 small squares for the 6. Design each digit inside its rectangle.

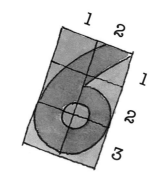

3 Decorate your digits with interesting colors and patterns. Now you can see the value of each digit in your two digit number at a glance.

5

8

HELPFUL HINTS
● For a number like 40 there are many rectangles that you could draw. You could choose a rectangle with two sides of 4 and two sides of 10, because 4x10=40 squares. You can draw any rectangle where the side lengths can be multiplied to make 40 squares. Sides of 5 and 8 are also possible because 5x8=40 squares.

MORE IDEAS
● Find some more paper with very small squares. Instead of just having a rectangular area for your digit, cut out the correct number of squares in any shape and design your digit inside the shape.

● You could color in the number of squares you need to make your digit. So for the 3 of 30 color in 30 squares.

PLACE YOUR DIGITS

Numbers can have any amount of digits! 841 is a three digit number. The first digit shows how many hundreds there are. The 8 has the value of eight hundred. If you rearrange the digits like this — 481 — the 8 has the value of eighty. What value does the 8 have in the number 418?

THREE CARD TRICK
You can play this game with one or two friends.

1 Using colored cardboard make a score card like the one on this page. Now make a set of cards, draw on the digits 1 to 9. Everyone takes three cards.

2 Rearrange your cards. What is the largest number you can make? The player who has the largest number scores a point.

3 What is the smallest number you can make? The player with the smallest number scores a point.

4 On the scorecard write down as many different numbers as you can make with your three cards. Score a point for each number.

5 Place the numbers in order from the smallest to the largest. Score an extra bonus point for doing this correctly. Could this player have scored more points?

3 CARD TRICK

Digit	5	2	6	points
Largest Number 652				1
Smallest Number 256				1
Different Numbers 625				1
562				1
256				1
652				1
Smallest to Largest 256				
562				
625				1
652				
Total Points				7

HELPFUL HINTS

● When comparing numbers with the same amount of digits to find which is larger, look at the digits on the left side of the number first. The larger the digit the larger the number. If the digit is the same then compare the next one. Repeat this until you find the larger number.

5 4 6 8

Thousands — Tens
Hundreds — Ones

MORE IDEAS

● The 5 in 5,468 has a value of five thousand. How many different numbers can you make with these four digits?

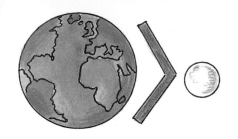

BIG, BIGGER, BIGGEST

Mathematicians use signs to show when a number is smaller or bigger than another number. They are called **inequality signs** and they look like this < or like this >. Whatever is on the open side is larger. For example 10>5.

HI SCORE!
You can play Hi Score on your own or with lots of friends. The object of the game is to make the number on the right of the scorecard as large as you can. This three digit number is your Hi Score.

HI SCORE

Player 1

Player 2

Player 3

Player 4

1 Copy this Hi Score game board. You could make it with colored cardboard and magic marker. Put your name and your friends' names in as the players.

2 Take turns to throw a die. Think carefully about where to place the digit you have thrown. You can't change it later.

3 Each line on the scorecard is a mathematical sentence. You only score if the sentence is true! If your digits were like this 621>451>233 you would score 233. If the numbers were not in the correct order like this 631>423>551 you would score nothing!

HELPFUL HINTS

● The most important digit is the one you put in the hundreds place. If you roll a 6 where would be the best place to put it?

● The number on the open side of the inequality sign, is always the larger one.

BIGGER > smaller

MORE IDEAS

● Invent a game called Lo Score. What will your board look like? Can you write out the rules to go with it? What number would be best to put in the hundreds place of the first column?

SIGN OF THE TIMES

Multiplying numbers is a quick way of adding the same number many times.

That's why some people say "times" to mean multiplication. The multiplication sign looks like this x. If we want to figure out what six 2s are, we don't need to write 2+2+2+2+2+2. We can write 6x2 instead.

MOUNTAIN MULTIPLICATION
Climb the mountain to find the number at the peak.

1 Cut out a triangle of cardboard and draw four "rocks" along the bottom, three rocks in the next row and two rocks in the third row. Cut out some "snow" and stick it on the peak.

3 Add poster putty to the back of each circle and stick the first four onto the bottom row. To find the next number up the mountain, multiply the two numbers below it.

2 Stick two triangles on the back for support and make trees for the sides. Cut out ten small circles of paper and write the numbers 2, 1, 2, 3 on the first four circles.

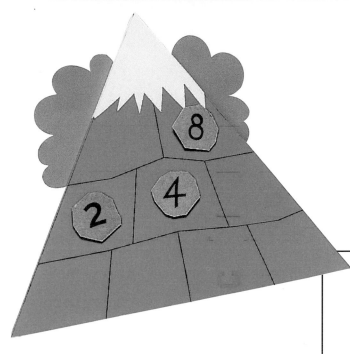

HELPFUL HINTS

● To find the number that is missing underneath the 8 (left), it can be helpful to think about it as a multiplication problem like this...

$$4 \times ? = 8$$

4 The number above the 2 and 1 will be 2 because 2x1=2. Figure out what all three numbers are on the next row.

5 Write them on the circles and stick them on. Keep repeating this, until you reach the top.

MORE IDEAS

● Can you figure out all the numbers that cover the mountain (above left) if you only have some of the numbers half way up the slope?

● Make your own mountain problem and get your friends to reach the top.

● Put 13 at the peak. Fill in the numbers on the mountain. What do you notice?

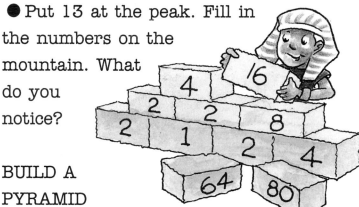

BUILD A PYRAMID

● Put some small numbers on four blocks. These are the base of your pyramid. Multiply the numbers as you did on the mountain and stick the answers on the next layer of blocks. Find the number at the top of the pyramid.

DO THE OPPOSITE

Have your parents ever said that you always do the opposite of what they tell you? When this happens in mathematics, it is called the inverse. The inverse of adding 3 is taking away 3. Do you know the inverse of multiplying by 2? Yes! **Dividing** by 2. What is the inverse of dividing by 4?

WHAT'S THAT NUMBER?

1 Cut some cardboard into small strips about as big as the one in the picture. Fold each strip to make three sections. Shade in the middle section lightly with a colored pencil.

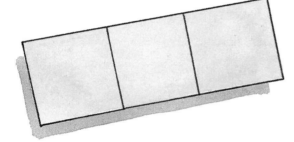

2 Next, choose a multiplication problem such as 3x8=24. The numbers 3 and 8 are the **factors.** The answer, 24, is the **product.**

3 Write the product in the middle square and the factors on either side. Make a pile of about 20 cards like this with different multiplication problems on each.

4 The first player picks up a card and folds one of the factors behind. The second player tries to figure out what the hidden number is. If they are correct, they win the card. Keep going until one player has all the cards.

MORE IDEAS
● You could play the same game with more difficult numbers.

HANDS DOWN
● This is another good game that you can play using factors and products. Instead of folding over a factor, cover one of the numbers with your hand. You could cover either the product or one of the factors on each side. Can your friends guess what number is hidden?

HARD TIMES!

Being able to remember multiplication facts quickly is very useful when trying to solve number problems. You can try to memorize the tables from the chart at the back of the book. But, here are some games that make learning your times tables much more fun!

CARD TRICKS

This is a game for two or more players. You will need a deck of cards with all the face cards removed.

1 Place the cards face down on the table. Choose a multiplication table, for example, the four times table.

2 Now, take turns to look at two cards. Is the product of the two numbers on the cards in the four times table?

3 If it is, keep the pair and take another turn. If not, turn the cards back over, it's the next player's turn. The winner is the player with the most pairs.

4 You could keep the cards 2 and 6 and have another turn. Could you keep the 3 and 7?

CHICKEN RACE

The object of this game is to make the biggest score you can.

1 You will need a die, a calculator, and a pencil and paper to draw out the chart. The first player throws the die and makes a note of the number.

2 Throw the die again and multiply the two numbers together. Keep throwing the die, multiplying the number on the die with your total. You must decide when to stop because... if a 1 is thrown, you get 0 for that turn! Use a calculator to check that your multiplication is correct.

Dare you keep throwing the die... or are you chicken?!

SCORING
CHICKEN RACE
You could note your
scores like this —

But things
could
go wrong...

3	
	x4
12	
	x2
24	
	x5
120	**stay!**
4	
	x2
8	
	x1 no
	score!

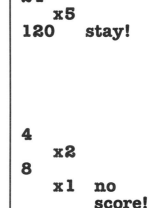

BIG TIME OPERATOR

If you have tried the other activities in this book, you will know more about addition, subtraction, multiplication, division, inverses, sums, factors and products than when you started! Are you skillful enough to use what you know to solve some of these number explosion problems?

NUMBER EXPLOSIONS

1 How many ways can you make 10? You have probably already thought of quite a few ways of making 10 by adding a couple of single digit numbers. But can you think of more interesting ways of making 10?

2 x 4 + 2 →

1 + 8 + 1 →

10

What about adding three numbers to make 10...

2 Use bright colored cardboard to design a huge explosion like the one in the picture and put 10 or any number you choose in the middle.

HELPFUL HINTS

● It is easy to be a big time operator and use all the operations if you remember some simple facts about the operations:

addition is the inverse of subtraction
multiplication is the inverse of division

How about adding a number then subtracting another?

● What happens when you add or subtract 0?
● What happens when you divide or multiply by 1?
● What happens if you multiply or divide by 0?

1 + 12 - 3

Try starting from 1,000. Can you add, divide, subtract then multiply a number to make 10?

FURTHER IDEAS

● How can you use the numbers 1, 2, 3, and 4 once each to make 10? One easy way is to add them all together 1+2+3+4=10.
● Use different operations and find other ways to make 10?

1+2+3+4 → 10

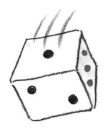

GAMES GALORE!

How many board games do you know? Which is your favorite? Some of the games in the book need you to use addition, subtraction, multiplication and division. Some games use dice, spinners, cards, and pieces. Can you invent your own game?

DESIGN YOUR OWN GAME

1 You might need pencils, pens, cardboard, something to make the pieces with — it all depends on the game you want to make. How creative can you be?

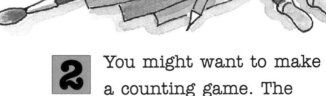

2 You might want to make a counting game. The game might need some cards that give the players different directions like "Go to Jail!" or "Start Again."

3 Decide who the game is going to be for: yourself, some adults, a friend, or a little brother or sister... don't make it too hard if it's for your little brother or sister!

4 Now give your game a theme — it could be animals or sports — what about space?

5 Now write down the rules. What do you have to do to win? Can you think of an exciting name?

1

2 — TRIP OVER ROCK. GO TO 12÷3

HAVE ANOTHER TURN

13

3 — LOSE TURN

12 — LOSE TURN

SEE MARS FOSSIL. GO TO 25–15

19

14

4

11 — RUN AWAY FROM METEOR. GO TO 7x2

20

15

FIND FOOT-PRINT. GO TO 5x2

18

THINK YOU SEE MARTIAN. GO TO 12+5

5

10

SUN TOO HOT. GO TO 4+2

17

16

RUN AWAY FROM DUST STORM. GO TO 20÷2

9

CAUGHT IN DUST STORM. GO TO 10–6

8

6

RETURN TO ROCKET FOR MORE OXYGEN AND START AGAIN

7

FIND THE MARTIAN!
This game is for 2–4 players. You will need a die, a piece for each player, and a calculator to check the answers to the problems.

Throw the die and move your piece. If you land on a question, you must answer it. The winner is the first person to reach the Martian.

PROBLEMS, PROBLEMS...

When you have a problem to solve, like finding out how many hairs you have on your head, the best way to tackle it is to make a careful guess, or an estimate, of the answer. Then, while you are tackling the problem, keep a note of any calculations you make. This will help you to check back if you make a mistake.

A NOVEL IDEA

1 Try to work out how many pages there are in a very thick book without looking at the page numbers!

Make an estimate. What do you think... 100, 325, 809?

3 You can look at the page numbers to check your answer. Can you think of a better way of solving the problem?

2 You could count the number of pages in one chapter. Next find the number of chapters. Now multiply the number of pages in a chapter by the number of chapters. This will give you an answer.

PARTY ANIMALS

1 If you have a party for your friends you will need to make some calculations. How many friends will be coming? Will you have ice cream?

2 What will it cost? How much allowance do you have? Is it enough? What do you need to buy? Do you need a loan from your parents?

Price of zoo ticket	$7.50
Number of friends	4
Total cost of tickets	$ ____
Allowance	$15.00
Need loan of	$ ____

3 Keep a careful note of the costs and how much you have spent.

GO FOR BROKE

Imagine you have just won a million dollars — but you have to spend it within one week! What would you spend it on?

1 Find some catalogs and magazines and decide how you are going to spend the money.

2 You need to prove that you have spent all the money in one week. How are you going to show that you have spent all that money?

RECEIPT

SPORTS CAR

$30,000

TIMES TABLES

1x1=1	1x4=4	1x7=7	1x10=10
2x1=2	2x4=8	2x7=14	2x10=20
3x1=3	3x4=12	3x7=21	3x10=30
4x1=4	4x4=16	4x7=28	4x10=40
5x1=5	5x4=20	5x7=35	5x10=50
6x1=6	6x4=24	6x7=42	6x10=60
7x1=7	7x4=28	7x7=49	7x10=70
8x1=8	8x4=32	8x7=56	8x10=80
9x1=9	9x4=36	9x7=63	9x10=90
10x1=10	10x4=40	10x7=70	10x10=100
11x1=11	11x4=44	11x7=77	11x10=110
12x1=12	12x4=48	12x7=84	12x10=120
1x2=2	1x5=5	1x8=8	1x11=11
2x2=4	2x5=10	2x8=16	2x11=22
3x2=6	3x5=15	3x8=24	3x11=33
4x2=8	4x5=20	4x8=32	4x11=44
5x2=10	5x5=25	5x8=40	5x11=55
6x2=12	6x5=30	6x8=48	6x11=66
7x2=14	7x5=35	7x8=56	7x11=77
8x2=16	8x5=40	8x8=64	8x11=88
9x2=18	9x5=45	9x8=72	9x11=99
10x2=20	10x5=50	10x8=80	10x11=111
11x2=22	11x5=55	11x8=88	11x11=121
12x2=24	12x5=60	12x8=96	12x11=132
1x3=3	1x6=6	1x9=9	1x12=12
2x3=6	2x6=12	2x9=18	2x12=24
3x3=9	3x6=18	3x9=27	3x12=36
4x3=12	4x6=24	4x9=36	4x12=48
5x3=15	5x6=30	5x9=45	5x12=60
6x3=18	6x6=36	6x9=54	6x12=72
7x3=21	7x6=42	7x9=63	7x12=84
8x3=24	8x6=48	8x9=72	8x12=96
9x3=27	9x6=54	9x9=81	9x12=108
10x3=30	10x6=60	10x9=90	10x12=120
11x3=33	11x6=66	11x9=99	11x12=132
12x3=36	12x6=72	12x9=108	12x12=144

GLOSSARY

Addition
When you use addition, two or more numbers are put together to find their total. The addition sign looks like this +, so 6+4=10.

Arithmetic
Arithmetic is the art of calculating with numbers. You use arithmetic when you solve number problems using addition, subtraction, multiplication, and division.

Division
Division is the opposite or inverse of multiplication. You could use division to find out how many 2s there are in 12. The division sign looks like this ÷ , so 12÷2=6.

Equals
The equals sign looks like this =. Whatever is on one side of the equals sign has to be the same amount as on the other side. Both sides must balance, so 7−1=3+1+2.

Factor
In multiplication, the numbers that you multiply together are the factors, so 6 and 2 are factors of 12.

Inequality sign
The inequality sign shows that one number is bigger or smaller than another. It looks like this < or like this >. Whatever is on the open side is larger, so 10>5.

Multiplication
Multiplication is a way of adding the same number many times. The sign looks like this x. Six 2s can be written like this 2+2+2+2+2+2 or like this 6x2, so 6x2=12.

Product
The product is the number you get when you multiply other numbers together, so 12 is the product of 6x2.

Subtraction
Subtraction is the opposite of addition. When you subtract you take one number away from another to find their difference. The subtraction sign is sometimes known as minus and looks like this −, so 10−4=6.

Sum
The sum is the total of a list of numbers that have been added together, so the sum of 3+2+4 is 9. We often use the word sum to describe any kind of number problem.

INDEX

addition 5, 6, 8, 24, 25, 26, 31
arithmetic 6, 8, 31

Black Spot 10-11

calculations 5, 28, 29, 31
calculators 11, 23, 27
cards 8–9, 20–21, 22, 25, 26
computer games 5
counters 8-9, 10-11, 26, 27
counting 5, 28

dice 6–7, 17, 23, 26, 27
digits 12–13, 14–15, 24
division 5, 20, 24, 25, 26, 31

equals 7, 31
estimates 28

faces 7, 22
factors 20, 21, 24, 31

facts 6, 7, 23, 25

games 5, 7, 8, 9, 10, 11, 14, 16, 20, 21, 26, 27

hundreds 14, 15, 17

inequality 16-17
inverses 20–21, 24, 25, 31

mathematicians 16
multiplication 5, 18, 20, 21, 22, 24, 25, 26, 31

opposites 20–21, 31

paper 6, 13, 18, 23
patterns 7, 11
pencils 6, 12, 20, 23, 26
pens 12, 16, 26
pirates 10, 11
problems 8, 19, 22, 24, 27, 28, 31
product 20, 21, 24, 31
projects 5

puzzles 31

questions 27

rectangles 12, 13
rockets 5, 27
rules 17, 26-27

signs 17, 31
solving 7, 28
spinners 26
squares 12, 13, 21
subtraction 5, 10, 11, 24, 25, 26, 31
sums 8, 31
summing up 8, 9
Sweet Sixteen 11

tables 22, 30
taking turns 10, 17, 22
thousands 15
totals 8, 9, 31
tricks 7, 14, 22